Editor

Gisela Lee

Editorial Manager

Karen J. Goldfluss, M.S. Ed.

Editor-in-Chief

Sharon Coan, M.S. Ed.

Cover Artist

Jessica Orlando

Art Coordinator

Denice Adorno

Creative Director

Elayne Roberts

Imaging

James Edward Grace

Product Manager

Phil Garcia

Publisher

Mary D. Smith, M.S. Ed.

W9-ATJ-673

How to Work with
Fractions,
Decimals & Percents

Grades 4–6

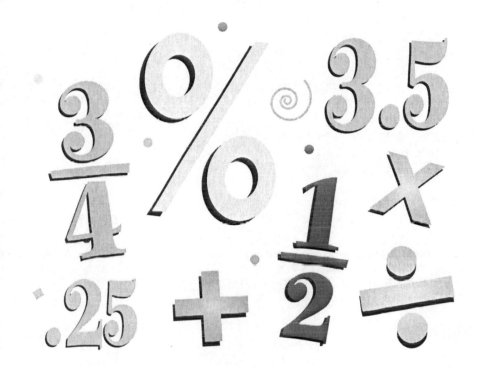

Author

Charles Shields

Teacher Created Resources, Inc.

12621 Western Avenue

Garden Grove, CA 92841

www.teachercreated.com

ISBN: 978-1-57690-955-3

©2000 Teacher Created Resources, Inc.

Reprinted, 2018

Made in U.S.A.

Table of Contents

A Note to Teachers and Parents

Welcome to the "How to" math series! You have chosen one of over two dozen books designed to give your children the information and practice they need to acquire important concepts in specific areas of math. The goal of the "How to" math books is to give children an extra boost as they work toward mastery of the math skills established by the National Council of Teachers of Mathematics (NCTM) and outlined in grade-level scope and sequence guidelines.

The design of this book is intended to allow it to be used by teachers or parents for a variety of purposes and needs. Each of the units contains one or more "How to" pages and one or more practice pages. The "How to" section of each unit precedes the practice pages and provides needed information such as a concept or math rule review, important terms and formulas to remember, and/or step-by-step guidelines necessary for using the practice pages. While most "How to" pages are written for direct use by the children, in some lower-grade-level books, these pages are presented as instructional pages or direct lessons to be used by a teacher or parent prior to introducing the practice pages.

About This Book

The activities in this book will help your children learn new skills or reinforce skills already learned in the following areas:

- developing concepts of fractions, mixed numbers, decimals, and percents
- developing number sense for fractions and decimals
- using models to relate fractions to decimals and to find equivalent fractions
- using models to explore operations with fractions, decimals, and percents
- applying fractions, decimals, and percents to problem situations

Fractions, decimals, and percents are an important extension of children's understanding of numbers. With these concepts in hand, children are prepared for the next step: applying fractions, decimals, and percents to real-world phenomena involving measurement, probability, and statistics.

How to Work with Fractions, Decimals, & Percents: Grades 4–6 presents a comprehensive, step-by-step overview of these fundamental mathematical concepts with clear, simple, readable instructional activities. The 12 units in this book can be used in whole-class instruction with the teacher or by a parent assisting his or her child with the concepts and exercises.

This book also lends itself to use by small groups doing remedial or review work on fractions, decimals, and percents, or for children and small groups in earlier grades engaged in enrichment or advanced work. Finally, this book can be used in a learning center with materials specified for each unit of instruction.

If children have difficulty on a specific concept or unit in this book, review the material and allow them to redo pages that are difficult for them. Since step-by-step concept development is essential, it's best not to skip sections of the book. Even if children find a unit easy, mastering the problems will build their confidence as they approach more difficult concepts.

Make available simple manipulatives to reinforce concepts. Use pennies, buttons, a ruler, beans, and similar materials to show proportions and ratios. Many children can grasp a numerical concept much more easily if they see it demonstrated.

This book is designed to match the standards of the National Council of Teachers of Mathematics. The standards strongly support the learning of fractions, decimals, percents, and other basic processes in the context of problem solving and real-world applications. Use every opportunity to have students apply these new skills in classroom situations and at home. This will reinforce the value of the skill as well as the process. This book matches a number of NCTM standards including the following main topics and specific features.

Concepts of Fractions, Mixed Numbers, Decimals, and Percents

Understanding the relationship between fractions, mixed numbers, decimals, and percents is a key step toward understanding more advanced concepts. This book carefully develops the step-by-step processes of renaming improper fractions as mixed numbers, for example, or of renaming fractions as decimals and percents. In addition, word problems involving practical applications of these concepts reinforce them.

Number Sense for Fractions, Decimals, and Percents

Learning numbers and their meaning in concrete, physical ways is emphasized in this book. Many examples involve determining parts of whole objects, or a percentage of time or money, for example, for the purpose of relating basic arithmetic operations to real-world problems.

Relating Fractions to Decimals and Finding Equivalencies

Students need to know fractions, decimals, and percents in relationship to other numbers and concepts. Students will learn how to express amounts in several ways, all of which represent equivalent amounts. As a result, students will learn how to approach a problem in more than one way.

Mathematical Connections Between Fractions, Decimals, and Percents

The instructions in this book emphasize the connections between ideas in mathematics. Illustrations reinforce the importance of understanding that a portion of something may be expressed in several ways or determined in several ways without sacrificing accuracy.

Problem Solving with Fractions, Decimals, and Percents

In this book a concept will frequently be introduced first as a practical problem—how to divide Halloween candy equally among an unknown number of bags, for instance. The skills students learn through these examples are further elaborated in the word problem section. Students will find that their confidence in recognizing essential information in problem solving grows stronger.

Other Standards

This book aligns well with other standards that focus on teaching computational skills, such as division and multiplication within the context of measurement and geometry. Students are also encouraged to use estimation to determine a reasonable answer, a skill often called for on standardized tests.

Facts to Know

A **fraction** describes part of a whole or part of a group of things. The bottom number of a fraction—the **denominator**—tells how many equal parts there are in the whole or group. The top number—the **numerator**—tells how many of the equal parts are being talked about.

numerator   **3** (shaded number of objects)
denominator   **4** (total number of objects)

Look at this fraction by itself:

$$\frac{2}{3} \quad \text{(2 is the numerator)} \atop \text{(3 is the denominator)}$$

In the fraction $\frac{4}{5}$, what is the numerator? What is the denominator?

The numerator is 4. The denominator is 5.

What are fractions used to describe?

✦ Use Fractions to Describe Part of a Whole.

Sample A

Mr. Olsen is planting his garden. He divides his garden into eight sections. Look at the chart below. What fraction describes the sections of his garden he plants with tomatoes?

tomatoes	tomatoes	peppers	peppers
tomatoes	beans	beans	onions

3 numerator (number of sections planted with tomatoes)
8 denominator (total number of equal sections of the garden)

You say "three-eighths"; you write $\frac{3}{8}$.
Mr. Olsen is planting $\frac{3}{8}$ of his garden with tomatoes.

✦ Use Fractions to Describe Parts of a Group.

Sample B

What part of the balloons are shaded?

3 numerator (number of shaded balloons)
6 denominator (total number of balloons)   

You say "three-sixths"; you write $\frac{3}{6}$.

Each balloon is $\frac{1}{6}$.

Six balloons are $\frac{6}{6}$ or the whole.

Facts to Know

You can find equivalent fractions by visualizing what they look like and comparing them. Look at the shapes on the right. How much of each one is shaded?

One-half of each shape is shaded. You say "one-half"; you write $\frac{1}{2}$.

A fraction such as $\frac{1}{2}$ can be renamed as different fractions with the same value. Look at it this way:

$$1 \qquad \frac{1}{2} \qquad \frac{1}{4} \quad + \quad \frac{1}{4} \quad = \quad \frac{2}{4} = \frac{1}{2}$$

As you can see from the pictures above, $\frac{2}{4}$ names the same amount as $\frac{1}{2}$. Look at some

other ways to name the same amount as $\frac{1}{2}$.

 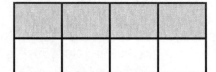

$$\frac{3}{6} = \frac{1}{2} \qquad\qquad \frac{4}{8} = \frac{1}{2} \qquad\qquad \frac{6}{12} = \frac{1}{2}$$

Fractions that name the same number or amount are called **equivalent fractions.**

There are many more equivalent fractions than ones that name the same number or amount as $\frac{1}{2}$.

  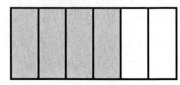

$$\frac{4}{6} = \frac{2}{3} \qquad\qquad \frac{4}{6} = \frac{2}{3} \qquad\qquad \frac{4}{6} = \frac{2}{3}$$

Four parts of the six are shaded. You say "four-sixths"; you write $\frac{4}{6}$. As a fraction, $\frac{2}{3}$ is equivalent to $\frac{4}{6}$.

To find equivalent fractions, multiply or divide the numerator and the denominator by the same number.

multiplication

$$\frac{2 \times 2 = 4}{3 \times 2 = 6} \text{ (numerator)} \atop \text{(denominator)}$$

division

$$\frac{4 \div 2 = 2}{6 \div 2 = 3} \text{ (numerator)} \atop \text{(denominator)}$$

Directions: Write the fraction for the part that is shaded. Determine whether the fraction is part of a whole or part of a group.

1.

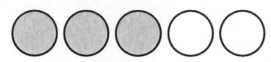

   a. The fraction is _____.
   b. The fraction is part of a _____.

3.

   a. The fraction is _____.
   b. The fraction is part of a _____.

2.

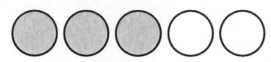

   a. The fraction is _____.
   b. The fraction is part of a _____.

4.

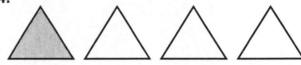

   a. The fraction is _____.
   b. The fraction is part of a _____.

Directions: Look at each chart and answer each question.

Seven-Day Triathlon Exercise Program

Day 1 run	Day 2 bike	Day 3 swim	Day 4 run	Day 5 bike	Day 6 rest	Day 7 swim

5. What fraction describes the part of the program for rest? _____.

Friday Class Schedule
(Each class is one hour long)

8:00 A.M. →	homework grading
9:00 A.M. →	math
10:00 A.M. →	vocabulary
11:00 A.M. →	science
Noon →	lunch
1:00 P.M. →	language arts
2:00 P.M. →	vocabulary
3:00 P.M. →	school ends for the day

Noon-Hour Schedule

12:00 P.M.–12:20 P.M. free time in gym
12:20 P.M.–12:40 P.M. lunch
12:40 P.M.–1:00 P.M. silent reading

6. What fraction describes the part of the day for vocabulary? _____.

7. What fraction describes the part of the hour for silent reading? _____.

Directions: Write the fraction beside each picture.

8.  _____

9. _____

10.  _____

Directions: Circle the fraction in each group that is equivalent to $\frac{1}{2}$.

1.   **a.** $\frac{1}{4}$ **b.** $\frac{2}{4}$ **c.** $\frac{2}{3}$

2.   **a.** $\frac{7}{14}$ **b.** $\frac{2}{6}$ **c.** $\frac{3}{9}$

3.   **a.** $\frac{6}{9}$ **b.** $\frac{9}{18}$ **c.** $\frac{9}{12}$

4.   **a.** $\frac{1}{4}$ **b.** $\frac{12}{24}$ **c.** $\frac{12}{36}$

5.   **a.** $\frac{8}{14}$ **b.** $\frac{14}{26}$ **c.** $\frac{10}{20}$

Directions: Multiply.

6. $\frac{3}{7} = \frac{}{21}$ By what was 7 multiplied to get 21? _____
                    What is the missing numerator? _____

7. $\frac{4}{9} = \frac{}{18}$ By what was 9 multiplied to get 18? _____
                    What is the missing numerator? _____

8. $\frac{2}{3} = \frac{}{18}$ By what was 3 multiplied to get 18? _____
                    What is the missing numerator? _____

9. $\frac{2}{5} = \frac{}{10}$ By what was 5 multiplied to get 10? _____
                    What is the missing numerator? _____

Directions: Divide.

10. $\frac{9}{12} = \frac{}{4}$ By what was 12 divided to get 4? _____
                    What is the missing numerator? _____

11. $\frac{8}{16} = \frac{}{2}$ By what was 16 divided to get 2? _____
                    What is the missing numerator? _____

12. $\frac{10}{24} = \frac{}{12}$ By what was 24 divided to get 12? _____
                    What is the missing numerator? _____

Directions: Which fraction (a, b, or c) is not equivalent to the given fraction?

13. $\frac{2}{3}$ **a.** $\frac{2}{6}$ **b.** $\frac{6}{9}$ **c.** $\frac{8}{12}$

14. $\frac{1}{5}$ **a.** $\frac{3}{15}$ **b.** $\frac{2}{10}$ **c.** $\frac{1}{10}$

15. $\frac{4}{7}$ **a.** $\frac{12}{21}$ **b.** $\frac{6}{14}$ **c.** $\frac{20}{35}$

Facts to Know

Common Factors (Greatest Common Factor, Composite Numbers, Prime Numbers)

A key to understanding operations involving fractions is knowing how to use factors.

Sample

Laura is making party-favor bags for the small children who are going to attend her son's party. She has 18 candy bars and 27 pieces of taffy. She wants to put the same number of pieces of candy into the bags. What is the greatest number of candy bars and taffy in the greatest number of bags?

You can experiment with different amounts, but the easiest way to solve the problem is to find the greatest common factor.

The **greatest common factor (GCF)** is the greatest factor a pair of numbers have in common.

List all of the factors of 18 and 27.

Factors of 18: 1, 2, 3, 6, ⑨, 18

Factors of 27: 1, 3, ⑨, 27

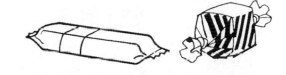

The greatest common factor is 9. Laura could have 9 bags with 2 candy bars (18 ÷ 9 = 2) and 3 pieces of taffy (27 ÷ 9 = 3) in each bag.

Numbers that have more than two factors to choose from, such as 18 and 27, are called **composite numbers**.

Some numbers have only two factors: 1 and the number itself. These are prime numbers. (1 is not considered composite or prime.)

Examples of prime numbers are 2, 3, 5, and 7.

To find prime and composite numbers under 50, use the chart below.

Step 1 → Cross out 1 because it is neither prime nor composite.
Step 2 → Circle 2, 3, 5, and 7. They are all prime.
Step 3 → Cross out all multiples of 2, 3, 5, and 7. What kinds of numbers are they?
Step 4 → Circle the remaining numbers. How many factors does each have?
   What kind of numbers are they?

1	2	3	4	5	6	7	8	9	10
11	12	13	14	15	16	17	18	19	20
21	22	23	24	25	26	27	28	29	30
31	32	33	34	35	36	37	38	39	40
41	42	43	44	45	46	47	48	49	50

Work with Simplest Form, Least Common Multiple, and Mixed Numbers

Facts to Know

Simplest Form

A fraction is in **simplest form** when the greatest common factor of the numerator and denominator is 1.

There are two methods of changing, or reducing, fractions to their simplest form.

✦ Find the greatest common factor.

> **Sample:** Simplify $\frac{8}{12}$.
>
> **Step 1** → Find the greatest common factor of 8 and 12.
>
> *Factors of 8:* 1, 2, ④
> *Factors of 12:* 1, 2, 3, ④, 6, 12
>
> The greatest common factor of 8 and 12 is 4.
>
> **Step 2** → Divide the numerator and denominator by the greatest common factor.
>
> $8 \div 4 = 2$
> $12 \div 4 = 3$
>
> The greatest common factor of 2 and 3 is 1.
>
> Therefore, $\frac{8}{12}$ equals $\frac{2}{3}$ in simplest form.

✦ Divide the numerator and denominator by any common factor until the greatest common factor of both is only 1.

> **Sample:** Simplify $\frac{18}{42}$.
>
> $$\frac{18 \div 3}{42 \div 3} = \frac{6 \div 2}{14 \div 2} = \frac{3}{7} \begin{array}{l} \text{(numerator)} \\ \text{(denominator)} \end{array}$$
>
> The greatest common factor of 3 and 7 is 1.
>
> Therefore, $\frac{18}{42}$ equals $\frac{3}{7}$ in simplest form.

Least Common Multiple (LCM)

A **multiple** is the product of two or more numbers. Knowing multiples will help you find answers to arithmetic problems.

Multiples of one number that are also multiples of another number are called **common multiples.**

> #### Sample
>
> Nina and Alex want to determine how many red and blue stage lights to order for the school play. They want two rows of lights: one of red and one of blue.
>
> Red lights come 3 in a box; blue lights come 4 in a box.
>
> But don't order a ton of lights!" the drama teacher says. "Get the least number of red and blue to make two even rows."
>
> How many boxes of each do they have to get to make two even rows?

Facts to Know

Least Common Multiple (LCM) *(cont.)*

Sample *(cont.)*

What you need to find is a common multiple of 3 and 4.

The smallest number that is a common multiple is called the **least common multiple (LCM)**. Learning how to find the least common multiple is important when you work with fractions.

Let's see where the least common multiple of 3 and 4 occurs.

Multiples of 3: 0, 3, 6, 9, (12), 15, 18

Multiples of 4: 0, 4, 8, (12), 16

The LCM is 12 because 4 boxes of 3 red lights is 12, and 3 boxes of 4 blue lights is 12.

> **Red = 4 boxes x 3 red lights in each box = 12 red lights**
>
> **Blue = 3 boxes x 4 blue lights in each box = 12 blue lights**

You can compare fractions by using the least common multiple to rename them as fractions with like denominators.

Sample: Compare $\frac{2}{3}$ and $\frac{3}{7}$. Which is larger?

Step 1 → Find the least common multiple of 3 and 7. It's 21.

Step 2 → Find equivalent fractions. (Remember, to find an equivalent fraction, multiply or divide the numerator and the denominator by the same number.) Because you are comparing two fractions ($\frac{2}{3}$ and $\frac{3}{7}$), use the least common multiple (21) as the denominator for both fractions.

$$\frac{2 \times 7}{3 \times 7} = \frac{14}{21} \qquad \frac{3 \times 3}{7 \times 3} = \frac{9}{21}$$

Step 3 → Compare the numerators to see which is larger. $\frac{14}{21} > \frac{9}{21} = \frac{2}{3} > \frac{3}{7}$

Mixed Numbers

What do you do when the numerator of a fraction is larger than the denominator? You write it as a mixed number. The numbers beneath the fraction number line show the concept of a mixed number.

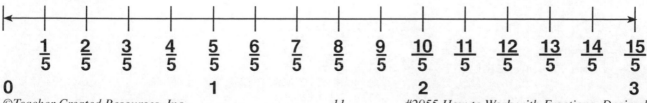

Facts to Know

Mixed Numbers *(cont.)*

A **mixed number** is a whole number with a fraction.

Some fractions can be renamed as a whole number only.

$$\frac{4}{4} \text{ or } 1 \quad + \quad \frac{4}{4} \text{ or } 1 \quad = \quad \frac{8}{4} \text{ or } 2$$

But in the fraction $\frac{5}{4}$, for instance, the numerator is greater than the denominator. Now what?

A fraction with a numerator greater than the denominator is an **improper fraction**.

You need to rename $\frac{5}{4}$, an improper fraction, as a mixed number.

$$\frac{4}{4} \quad + \quad \frac{1}{4} \quad = \quad \frac{5}{4} \quad = \quad 1\frac{1}{4}$$

To write an improper fraction as a mixed number or a whole number, you divide.

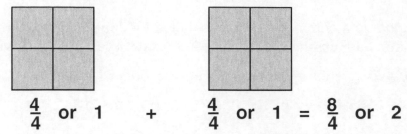

Step 1 ⟶ $\frac{18}{5} = 18 \div 5$

Step 2 ⟶ $5\overline{)18} \; \begin{array}{r} 3 \\ \hline 18 \\ -15 \\ \hline 3 \end{array}$ so $\frac{18}{5} = 3\frac{3}{5}$

On the other hand, to rename a mixed number as an improper fraction, multiply and add. On the number line on page 11, you can see that each $\frac{5}{5}$ is a whole. So to rename $2\frac{3}{5}$ as an improper fraction, you must multiply the whole number 2 by $\frac{5}{5}$ to find out how many fifths are in 2 wholes.

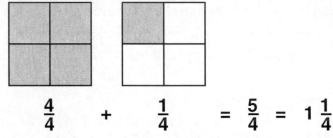

$$2\frac{3}{5} = 2 + \frac{3}{5} = \left(2 \times \frac{5}{5}\right) + \frac{3}{5} = \left(\frac{10}{5}\right) + \frac{3}{5} = \frac{13}{5}$$

Check the number line to see if this is correct.

Finally, to rename a whole number as a fraction, multiply the whole number by a name for 1, such as $\frac{1}{1}, \frac{2}{2}, \frac{3}{3}, \frac{4}{4}$ and so on.

Here's 2 with a denominator of 5 ⟶ $2 = 2 \times \frac{5}{5} = \frac{10}{5}$

Here's 4 with a denominator of 1 ⟶ $4 = 4 \times \frac{1}{1} = \frac{4}{1}$

Directions: Circle which fraction is not in simplest form.

1. a. $\frac{1}{7}$ b. $\frac{4}{8}$ c. $\frac{2}{5}$ d. $\frac{2}{7}$

2. a. $\frac{3}{4}$ b. $\frac{2}{9}$ c. $\frac{2}{7}$ d. $\frac{3}{9}$

3. a. $\frac{5}{6}$ b. $\frac{7}{11}$ c. $\frac{2}{12}$ d. $\frac{7}{9}$

4. a. $\frac{9}{11}$ b. $\frac{5}{15}$ c. $\frac{9}{17}$ d. $\frac{10}{13}$

5. a. $\frac{6}{8}$ b. $\frac{5}{9}$ c. $\frac{1}{22}$ d. $\frac{8}{33}$

6. a. $\frac{7}{22}$ b. $\frac{5}{21}$ c. $\frac{8}{20}$ d. $\frac{5}{8}$

Directions: Write each fraction in simplest form.

7. $\frac{18}{45} =$ _____   10. $\frac{6}{15} =$ _____   13. $\frac{16}{32} =$ _____

8. $\frac{30}{40} =$ _____   11. $\frac{9}{12} =$ _____   14. $\frac{20}{25} =$ _____

9. $\frac{12}{14} =$ _____   12. $\frac{15}{18} =$ _____   15. $\frac{14}{28} =$ _____

Directions: Find the least common multiple for each pair of numbers.

16. 2 _____   18. 6 _____   20. 4 _____

    5 _____   9 _____   6 _____

17. 3 _____   19. 8 _____   21. 5 _____

    7 _____   3 _____   8 _____

Directions: Circle the greater fraction in each pair.

22. $\frac{2}{5}$ $\frac{7}{15}$ 24. $\frac{5}{6}$ $\frac{3}{4}$ 26. $\frac{3}{4}$ $\frac{5}{8}$

23. $\frac{1}{2}$ $\frac{3}{8}$ 25. $\frac{2}{3}$ $\frac{4}{6}$ 27. $\frac{7}{8}$ $\frac{5}{6}$

Directions: Rename any improper fraction as a mixed number, any mixed number as an improper fraction, and any whole number as a fraction.

28. a. $1\frac{1}{5} =$ _____ b. $\frac{13}{4} =$ _____ c. $\frac{15}{7} =$ _____ d. $\frac{5}{3} =$ _____ e. $\frac{19}{8} =$ _____

29. a. $2\frac{1}{4} =$ _____ b. $6\frac{2}{3} =$ _____ c. $7\frac{3}{8} =$ _____ d. $1\frac{3}{4} =$ _____ e. $5\frac{3}{8} =$ _____

30. 3 with a denominator of 5 _____   33. 8 with a denominator of 3 _____

31. 5 with a denominator of 4 _____   34. 7 with a denominator of 7 _____

32. 2 with a denominator of 8 _____   35. 6 with a denominator of 5 _____

Facts to Know

Like and Unlike Fractions

Fractions that have the same denominators are called **like fractions** because their denominators are the same. You can think of it this way:

Numerators may be different.
Denominators are the same.

Using numbers in place of symbols, here's an example of like fractions:

Numerators may be different.
Denominators are the same. $\qquad \dfrac{3}{12} \quad \dfrac{2}{12} \quad \dfrac{4}{12} \quad \dfrac{6}{12} \quad \dfrac{8}{12}$

Fractions that have different denominators are called **unlike fractions** because their denominators are not the same.

Numerators may be different.
Denominators are different.

Numerators may be different.
Denominators are different. $\qquad \dfrac{7}{11} \quad \dfrac{3}{5} \quad \dfrac{5}{9}$

Adding and Subtracting Like Fractions

Adding like fractions is simple. Add the numerators only. Here's how to add like fractions in three steps:

Step 1 → Compare the denominators. Are the denominators the same? Then you have like denominators. $\qquad \dfrac{3}{8} + \dfrac{1}{8} = \dfrac{4}{8}$

Step 2 → Write the sum over the like denominator.

(Remember, add the numerators only.)

Step 3 → Simplify, if possible. $\dfrac{4}{8}$ can be simplified as $\dfrac{1}{2}$.

Note: If the sum of the numerators is greater than the denominator, then it is an improper fraction. Change it to a mixed number:

$$\dfrac{5}{12} + \dfrac{9}{12} = \dfrac{14}{12} \text{ (or as a mixed number) } 1\dfrac{2}{12} \text{ which can be simplified to } 1\dfrac{1}{6}$$

Subtracting like fractions follows the same three steps, only in Step 2 you subtract, not add, the numerators:

$$\dfrac{5}{9} - \dfrac{2}{9} = \dfrac{3}{9} \text{ (or simplified) } = \dfrac{1}{3}$$

Add and Subtract Like and Unlike Fractions and Mixed Numbers

Facts to Know

Adding and Subtracting Unlike Fractions

Adding unlike fractions means having to do an extra step.

Step 1→Compare the denominators.

$$\frac{4}{5} + \frac{2}{3} = ?$$

Are the denominators different? Then you have unlike fractions.

Step 2→(the extra step) Rewrite the fractions with like denominators (make them equivalent fractions, in other words). Always find the least common multiple for the denominator—smaller numbers are simpler to use.

The least common multiple of 3 and 5 is 15. (See page 11 for a review.)

$$\frac{4}{5} + \frac{2}{3} = \left(\frac{4}{5} \times \frac{3}{3}\right) + \left(\frac{2}{3} \times \frac{5}{5}\right)$$

Step 3→Write the sum of the numerators over the like denominator.

$$\frac{12}{15} + \frac{10}{15} = \frac{22}{15}$$

Step 4→Simplify, if possible.

$$\frac{22}{15} \text{ can be simplified as a mixed number } 1\frac{7}{15}$$

Subtracting unlike fractions follows the same four steps, except that in Step 3, you write the difference between the numerators over the like denominator.

Step 1→Compare the denominators. $\frac{10}{20} - \frac{2}{5} = ?$

Step 2→Rewrite with like denominators. $\frac{10}{20} - \frac{8}{20}$

Step 3→Subtract the numerators. Write the difference over the like denominator. $\frac{10}{20} - \frac{8}{20} = \frac{2}{20}$

Step 4→Simplify. $\frac{2}{20} = \frac{1}{10}$

Facts to Know

Adding Like and Unlike Mixed Numbers

A mixed number, you should remember from page 12, is a whole number with a fraction, such as $2\frac{1}{4}$.

But what do you do when you have to add two mixed numbers?

$$2\frac{1}{4} + 1\frac{3}{4} = ?$$

One way to think of this problem is to draw squares, so you can see a picture of it.

How many complete boxes can you get if you add the shaded parts together?

$$2\frac{1}{4}$$
$$+1\frac{3}{4}$$
_____
$$4$$

So, $2\frac{1}{4} + 1\frac{3}{4} = 4$. That was easy because both fractions had like denominators. Here's the step-by-step way to add mixed numbers with like denominators.

Step 1 → Add the numerators of the fractions.
  (Don't add the denominators!)

Step 2 → Add the whole numbers.

Step 3 → Simplify, if possible.

$$2\frac{2}{5}$$
$$+1\frac{1}{5}$$
_____
$$3\frac{3}{5}$$

Sometimes, though, you need to rename mixed numbers before you can add. You do this by regrouping, the same way you do when you add whole numbers.

Step 1 → Add numerators.   **Step 2** → Regroup.   **Step 3** → Simplify, if possible.

$$3\frac{6}{10}$$
$$+2\frac{8}{10}$$
_____
$$\frac{14}{10} = 1\frac{4}{10}$$

$$3\frac{6}{10}$$
$$+2\frac{8}{10}$$
_____
$$6\frac{4}{10}$$

$$6\frac{4}{10} = 6\frac{2}{5}$$

If you have unlike denominators, you must first turn them into like denominators, so you can add them. You may or may not have to regroup after you add the numerators.

Step 1 → Find like denominators.   **Step 2** → Add numerators.   **Step 3** → Regroup.

$$3\frac{3}{5} = 3\frac{9}{15}$$
$$+2\frac{2}{3} = 2\frac{10}{15}$$
_____

$$+3\frac{9}{15}$$
$$+2\frac{10}{15}$$
_____
$$\frac{19}{15} = 1\frac{4}{15}$$

$$+3\frac{9}{15}$$
$$+2\frac{10}{15}$$
_____
$$6\frac{4}{15}$$

Step 4 → Simplify, if possible. $6\frac{4}{15}$ is the simplest form.

Add and Subtract Like and Unlike Fractions and Mixed Numbers

Facts to Know

Subtracting Like and Unlike Mixed Numbers

To subtract mixed numbers, use the same methods you use to add them. But before you try to solve the problem, you should think about these two questions and answer yes to only one:

- If the problem has like denominators, do I have to regroup?
- If the problem has unlike denominators, do I have to regroup?

Subtracting mixed numbers with like denominators may or may not require regrouping. It depends on the numerators.

Rule: With like denominators, if the numerator in the subtrahend is smaller than the numerator in the minuend, subtract the numerators because you don't have to regroup.

$$3\frac{8}{12}$$
$$-2\frac{3}{12}$$
$$1\frac{5}{12}$$

Since 8 is greater than 3, you can subtract without regrouping.

If the second numerator is smaller than the first, you can subtract without regrouping

Rule: With like denominators, if the numerator in the subtrahend is greater than the numerator in the minuend, then you must regroup 1 from a whole number.

Now you can subtract.

Subtracting mixed numbers with unlike denominators may or may not require regrouping. Again, it depends on the numerator.

Rule: With unlike denominators, if—after you've found like denominators—the numerator after the minus sign is smaller than the first numerator, subtract the numerators. You do not have to regroup.

$$3\frac{3}{4} = 3\frac{9}{12}$$
$$-1\frac{1}{2} = 1\frac{6}{12}$$
$$2\frac{3}{12} = 2\frac{1}{4}$$

After finding the lowest common denominator and the new numerators, subtract without regrouping because 9 is larger than 6.

Rule: With unlike denominators, if—after you've found like denominators—the numerator after the minus sign is larger than the first numerator, you must regroup 1 from the whole number.

$$7\frac{1}{5} = 7\frac{3}{15}$$
$$4\frac{2}{3} = 4\frac{10}{15}$$

since 3 < 10, regroup by making $7\frac{3}{15}$ into $6\frac{18}{15}$

$$6\frac{18}{15}$$
$$-4\frac{10}{15}$$
$$2\frac{8}{15}$$

subtract the numbers

Adding and Subtracting Like and Unlike Fractions and Mixed Numbers

Directions: Use the information on pages 14–17 to complete the following problems. Add and subtract the like fractions. Remember to simplify when you can.

1. $\dfrac{3}{5} + \dfrac{1}{5} =$ 5. $\dfrac{9}{12} - \dfrac{6}{12} =$ 9. $\dfrac{6}{11} + \dfrac{7}{11} =$

2. $\dfrac{2}{7} + \dfrac{3}{7} =$ 6. $\dfrac{3}{21} + \dfrac{4}{21} =$ 10. $\dfrac{13}{7} - \dfrac{3}{7} =$

3. $\dfrac{1}{10} + \dfrac{1}{10} =$ 7. $\dfrac{3}{4} + \dfrac{3}{4} =$ 11. $\dfrac{5}{6} + \dfrac{2}{3} =$

4. $\dfrac{6}{14} - \dfrac{1}{14} =$ 8. $\dfrac{2}{15} + \dfrac{3}{15} =$ 12. $\dfrac{1}{4} + \dfrac{3}{8} =$

Directions: Add the mixed numbers. Remember to regroup when necessary. Always simplify, if possible.

13. $3\dfrac{2}{3} + 4\dfrac{2}{3} =$ 15. $\dfrac{1}{3} + 3\dfrac{1}{6} =$ 17. $3\dfrac{3}{5} + 5\dfrac{4}{5} =$

14. $4\dfrac{3}{7} + 2\dfrac{4}{7} =$ 16. $5\dfrac{6}{7} + 6\dfrac{3}{14} =$

Directions: Look at the problem. Answer the questions. Then subtract the mixed numbers.

18. $\begin{array}{r} 3\frac{2}{3} \\ -\,2\frac{1}{3} \\ \hline \end{array}$ Does the problem have like or unlike denominators? ☐ Like ☐ Unlike

Do I have to regroup to subtract? ☐ Yes ☐ No

19. $\begin{array}{r} 8\frac{1}{4} \\ -\,5\frac{3}{4} \\ \hline \end{array}$ Does the problem have like or unlike denominators? ☐ Like ☐ Unlike

Do I have to regroup to subtract? ☐ Yes ☐ No

20. $\begin{array}{r} 5\frac{5}{6} \\ -\,2\frac{2}{9} \\ \hline \end{array}$ Does the problem have like or unlike denominators? ☐ Like ☐ Unlike

Do I have to regroup to subtract? ☐ Yes ☐ No

Facts to Know

There is more than one way to multiply with fractions.

- You can multiply fractions by whole numbers.

    Example: Anna ran around the quarter-mile track twice. $\frac{1}{4}$ mile x 2

- You can multiply fractions by fractions.

    Example: Anna sprinted for half of the quarter-mile track. $\frac{1}{4}$ mile x $\frac{1}{2}$

- You can multiply fractions by mixed numbers.

    Example: Anna ran $6\frac{1}{2}$ times around the quarter-mile track. $6\frac{1}{2}$ x $\frac{1}{4}$ mile

Fractions and Whole Numbers

When you multiply a whole number by a fraction between 0 and 1, the product is less than the whole number you started with.

If a store has a half-off sale and an item costs $10, how much does it cost on sale?

10 x $\frac{1}{2}$ = $5. The product $5 is less than $10 because you multiplied by a fraction between 1 and 0.

Here's a way to use a picture to imagine what happens when you multiply a whole number by a fraction. If $\frac{2}{3}$ of a school of 24 fish went swimming for food, how many fish left to search for food?

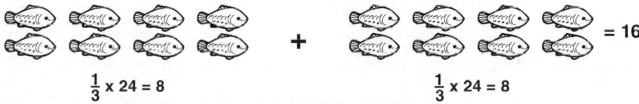

$\frac{1}{3}$ x 24 = 8 $\frac{1}{3}$ x 24 = 8   = 16

Here are the steps for multiplying a fraction by a whole number.

Sample: $\frac{3}{4}$ x 12

Step 1 → Write the whole number as a fraction. $\frac{3}{4}$ x 12 can be rewritten as $\frac{3}{4}$ x $\frac{12}{1}$

Step 2 → Multiply the numerators. Multiply the denominators. $\frac{3}{4}$ x $\frac{12}{1}$ = $\frac{36}{4}$

Step 3 → Simplify, if possible. $\frac{36}{4}$ = 9

When you multiply two fractions that are between 0 and 1, the product is smaller than both fractions. Imagine cutting a rectangle into fourths. Now you cut these fourths in half.

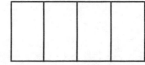 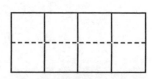

Half of that fourth is $\frac{1}{8}$ of the rectangle.

$\frac{1}{4}$ x $\frac{1}{2}$ = $\frac{1}{8}$

Facts to Know

Here are the steps for multiplying a fraction by a fraction.

Step 1 ⟶ Multiply the numerators. Multiply the denominators. $\frac{2}{3} \times \frac{3}{8} = \frac{6}{24}$

Step 2 ⟶ Simplify, if possible. $\frac{6}{24} \div \frac{6}{6} = \frac{1}{4}$

Mixed Numbers

When you multiply a positive mixed number by a fraction between 0 and 1, the product is less than the mixed number.

Sample A: $3\frac{3}{4} \times \frac{1}{3}$

Step 1 ⟶ Change the mixed number into an improper fraction. $3 = \frac{12}{4}$ so $\frac{12}{4} + \frac{3}{4} = \frac{15}{4}$

Step 2 ⟶ Multiply the numerators. Multiply the denominators. $\frac{15}{4} \times \frac{1}{3} = \frac{15}{12}$

Step 3 ⟶ Simplify, if possible. $\frac{15}{12} = \frac{5}{4} = 1\frac{1}{4}$

Sample B: $1\frac{3}{4} \times \frac{1}{5}$

Step 1 ⟶ Change the mixed number into an improper fraction. $1 = \frac{4}{4}$ so $\frac{4}{4} + \frac{3}{4} = \frac{7}{4}$

Step 2 ⟶ Multiply the numerators. Multiply the denominators. $\frac{7}{4} \times \frac{1}{5} = \frac{7}{20}$

Step 3 ⟶ Simplify, if possible. $\frac{7}{20}$ is in simplest form.

Multiplying Fractions, Whole Numbers, and Mixed Numbers

Directions: Multiply the fractions by whole numbers. Simplify, if possible.

1. $\frac{1}{3} \times 1 =$

2. $\frac{3}{4} \times 12 =$

3. $\frac{7}{8} \times 5 =$

4. $\frac{4}{11} \times 7 =$

5. Lauren has a $\frac{1}{2}$ gallon of lemonade mixed. She thinks she needs 6 times that much for the school picnic. How many gallons does she need?

6. The coach said to run twice around the quarter-mile track. How far do you have to run?

7. After the first game of the playoffs, half of the 20 teams were eliminated. After the second game, another half were eliminated. How many were left?

8. One-third of the class of 27 students has the flu. How many have the flu?

Directions: Multiply fractions by fractions. Simplify, if possible.

9. $\frac{2}{3} \times \frac{1}{5} =$

10. $\frac{7}{8} \times \frac{3}{6} =$

11. $\frac{2}{9} \times \frac{4}{7} =$

12. Andrew bought a piece of plywood $\frac{1}{4}$ inch thick. His grandpa said he really needed a piece only $\frac{1}{2}$ that thick. How thick would the right piece of plywood be?

13. Eli and Kathryn are painting the porch steps. They have three-quarters of a gallon of paint. "Give me half of that," says Eli. What fraction of the gallon does he want?

14. Coach Chen wants to divide the $\frac{1}{4}$ mile track into fourths so four teams can run sprints. What fraction of a mile will each section be?

15. "That mountain is half a mile high," said the guide. "No one's climbed higher than $\frac{1}{3}$ the way up." What fraction of a mile is that?

16. The recipe says to use $\frac{3}{4}$ cup of sugar. You are making only half the recipe. How much sugar should you use?

Directions: Multiply the mixed numbers and fractions. Remember to simplify, if possible.

17. $\frac{3}{6} \times 1\frac{2}{3} =$

20. $6\frac{1}{2} \times \frac{2}{3} =$

23. $\frac{1}{4} \times 3\frac{1}{5} =$

18. $2\frac{1}{3} \times \frac{3}{4} =$

21. $1\frac{1}{2} \times 6 =$

24. $2\frac{3}{8} \times \frac{4}{5} =$

19. $3\frac{3}{4} \times \frac{3}{5} =$

22. $\frac{5}{7} \times 3\frac{4}{5} =$

25. $3\frac{3}{4} \times \frac{1}{9} =$

Facts to Know

Reciprocals

The key to dividing with fractions is understanding reciprocals. A **reciprocal** is two numbers that have the product of one. Here are some examples:

$\frac{2}{3}$ and $\frac{3}{2}$ are reciprocals because $\frac{2}{3}$ x $\frac{3}{2}$ = $\frac{6}{6}$ or 1

$\frac{4}{1}$ and $\frac{1}{4}$ are reciprocals because $\frac{4}{1}$ x $\frac{1}{4}$ = $\frac{4}{4}$ or 1

$3\frac{1}{2}$ (or $\frac{7}{2}$) and $\frac{2}{7}$ are reciprocals because $\frac{7}{2}$ x $\frac{2}{7}$ = $\frac{14}{14}$ or 1

Knowing what a reciprocal is will be your key to understanding how to divide with fractions.

Dividing Fractions

Look at the sample problem below to see the two different ways to solve the same problem.

Sample

Clara had three apples. She wanted to share the apples with some of her friends. If she split each apple into thirds and each person gets a third, how many plates does she need?

First, draw 3 apples.

Then, divide the apples into thirds.

Count the number of thirds.

Clara needs 9 plates to divide 3 apples by thirds.   **x 9 = 9 plates**

Here's how to do the problem using numbers, not pictures.

Step 1 → Write the whole number as a fraction.   **$3 \div \frac{1}{3}$ is the same as $\frac{3}{1} \div \frac{1}{3}$**

Step 2 → Multiply the dividend by the reciprocal of the divisor. $\frac{3}{1} \div \frac{1}{3} = \frac{3}{1}$ x $\frac{3}{1}$ = 9

Step 3 → Simplify, if possible. $\frac{9}{1}$ = 9

5 How to •••••••••••••••••Divide with Fractions

Facts to Know

If you need to divide a fraction by a whole number, the steps are almost the same. Let's say you need to divide $\frac{3}{4}$ pounds of clay between 2 students in art class.

Sample A

Step 1 → Write the whole number as a fraction. $\frac{3}{4} \div 2$ **is the same as** $\frac{3}{4} \div \frac{2}{1}$

Step 2 → Multiply by the reciprocal of the divisor. $\frac{3}{4} \times \frac{1}{2} = \frac{3}{8}$

Step 3 → Simplify, if possible. $\frac{3}{8}$ is in simplest form

Dividing a fraction by a fraction involves only two steps.

Sample B

Miguel is building a kite. He has a piece of string $\frac{3}{4}$ yard long. Into how many $\frac{3}{8}$ yard pieces can he snip the string?

So the problem looks like this: $\frac{3}{4} \div \frac{3}{8} = ?$

Step 1 → Multiply the dividend by the reciprocal of the divisor. $\frac{3}{4} \div \frac{3}{8} = \frac{3}{4} \times \frac{8}{3} = \frac{24}{12}$

Step 2 → Simplify, if possible. $\frac{24}{12} = 2$

Shortcut for Dividing Fractions

You can use common factors to find a shortcut for dividing fractions. (It works for multiplying fractions, too!) Here's an example, using the problem $\frac{1}{3} \div \frac{1}{6}$

First, set up the problem up to multiply the dividend by the reciprocal of the divisor, as you would in Step 1 above.

$$\frac{1}{3} \div \frac{1}{6} = \frac{1}{3} \times \frac{6}{1}$$

Next, 3 is a factor of 3 and 6. Divide the numerator and denominator by 3. Multiply.

$$\frac{1}{\cancel{3}_1} \times \frac{\cancel{6}^2}{1} = \frac{2}{1} = 2$$

If you can divide fractions and mixed numbers, you can divide mixed numbers. What you have to do to the mixed number is the same.

Sample C

Jenny is making a birdhouse. She has a $5\frac{3}{4}$ foot-long board. How many $1\frac{1}{3}$ foot boards can she cut from the long board?

This problem looks like this: $5\frac{3}{4} \div 1\frac{1}{3} = ?$

Step 1 → Write the mixed numbers as fractions. $\qquad 5\frac{3}{4} = \frac{23}{4}$ and $1\frac{1}{3} = \frac{4}{3}$

Step 2 → Multiply by the reciprocal of the divisor. $\qquad \frac{23}{4} \times \frac{3}{4} = \frac{69}{16}$

Step 3 → Simplify, if possible. $\qquad \frac{69}{16} = 4\frac{5}{16}$

Directions: Write the reciprocal of each number.

1. 3 _____

2. $\frac{3}{4}$ _____

3. 5 _____

4. $\frac{8}{9}$ _____

5. 10 _____

6. 7 _____

7. $\frac{4}{5}$ _____

8. $\frac{6}{7}$ _____

9. 4 _____

10. 17 _____

Directions: Solve the problems. Remember to simplify, if possible.

11. $6 \div \frac{1}{3} =$

12. $\frac{3}{5} \div 4 =$

13. $5 \div \frac{5}{6} =$

14. $4 \div \frac{1}{8} =$

15. $6 \div \frac{8}{9} =$

16. $\frac{3}{4} \div 2 =$

17. $2 \div \frac{1}{3} =$

18. $5 \div \frac{1}{5} =$

19. $\frac{1}{3} \div 7 =$

20. $3 \div \frac{6}{9} =$

21. $\frac{3}{8} \div 12 =$

22. $\frac{11}{15} \div 4 =$

23. $\frac{7}{8} \div 3 =$

24. $5 \div \frac{2}{13} =$

25. $4 \div \frac{6}{7} =$

26. $6 \div \frac{7}{9} =$

27. $\frac{10}{13} \div 2 =$

28. $\frac{4}{5} \div 16 =$

29. $8 \div \frac{2}{3} =$

30. $\frac{7}{12} \div 7 =$

Directions: Solve the problems. Use the shortcut method when you see common factors. Simplify, if possible.

1. $\frac{1}{2} \div \frac{3}{5} =$

2. $\frac{1}{3} \div \frac{3}{4} =$

3. $\frac{3}{4} \div \frac{4}{5} =$

4. $\frac{6}{7} \div \frac{1}{3} =$

5. $\frac{1}{5} \div \frac{1}{2} =$

6. $\frac{1}{2} \div \frac{1}{8} =$

7. $\frac{3}{8} \div \frac{3}{4} =$

8. $\frac{1}{4} \div \frac{1}{4} =$

9. $\frac{4}{5} \div \frac{1}{5} =$

10. $\frac{7}{9} \div \frac{1}{3} =$

11. $1\frac{1}{2} \div 2\frac{1}{4} =$

12. $4\frac{3}{5} \div 2\frac{1}{2} =$

13. $5\frac{1}{2} \div 2\frac{6}{7} =$

14. $5\frac{3}{4} \div 2\frac{1}{2} =$

15. $2\frac{5}{6} \div 1\frac{2}{3} =$

16. $4\frac{5}{6} \div 2\frac{1}{3} =$

17. $2\frac{7}{8} \div 1\frac{3}{4} =$

18. $3\frac{2}{3} \div 1\frac{1}{5} =$

19. $2\frac{2}{5} \div 3\frac{1}{8} =$

20. $1\frac{3}{8} \div 1\frac{1}{2} =$

Facts to Know

In this unit you will learn how to express fractions as decimal numbers. **Decimal numbers** are numbers that are written using place value. A decimal point separates the whole-number places from the places that are less than one.

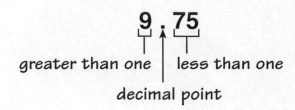

A review of place value will help you better understand decimal numbers.

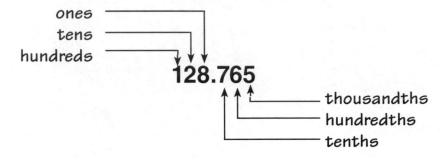

You need to know place value to compare and order decimal numbers. Follow the steps in the sample below.

Sample

If a rock weighs 2.347 lbs. and another weighs 2.349 lbs., which weighs more?

Step 1 ⟶ Compare the digits in the ones place.

2.347
2.349

(Both numbers have the same digit in the ones place.)

Step 2 ⟶ Compare the digits in the tenths place.

2.347
2.349

(Both numbers have the same digit in the tenths place.)

Step 3 ⟶ Compare the digits in the hundredths place.

2.347
2.349

(Both numbers have the same digit in the hundredths place.)

Step 4 ⟶ Compare the digits in the thousandths place.

2.347
2.349

(9 is greater than 7.)

Therefore, 2.349 > 2.347

6 ⟩ How to •••••••••• Add and Subtract Decimals

Facts to Know

Adding decimals is the same as adding whole numbers. The key is to line up the decimal points correctly.

Adding Whole Numbers and Numbers with Decimals

When adding whole numbers, you follow these steps.

> **Sample: 23,408 + 6,594 = ?**
>
> **Step 1** ⟶ For whole numbers, line up the digits.
>
> **Step 2** ⟶ Add and regroup, as needed.

$$\begin{array}{r} 23{,}408 \\ +\ 6{,}594 \\ \hline 30{,}002 \end{array}$$

When adding decimals, follow these steps.

> **Sample: 62.34 + 2.8 = ?**
>
> **Step 1** ⟶ For decimals, line up the decimal points.
>
> **Step 2** ⟶ Add and regroup, as needed.

$$\begin{array}{r} 62.34 \\ +\ 2.8 \\ \hline 65.14 \end{array}$$

Subtracting Whole Numbers and Numbers with Decimals

Subtracting decimals is the same as subtracting whole numbers. Once again, the key is to line up the decimal points correctly.

When subtracting whole numbers, follow these steps.

> **Sample: 763 − 25 = ?**
>
> **Step 1** ⟶ For whole numbers, line up the digits.
>
> **Step 2** ⟶ Subtract and regroup as needed.

$$\begin{array}{r} {}^{5\,1}\!\!\!\!\!\\ 7\cancel{6}3 \\ -\ 25 \\ \hline 738 \end{array}$$

When subtracting decimals follow these steps.

> **Sample: 61.3 − 2.89 = ?**
>
> **Step 1** ⟶ For decimals, line up the decimal points.
>
> **Step 2** ⟶ *Optional:* If necessary, add zeros for any empty number places when regrouping is needed. In this example, a zero is needed in the hundredths place for 61.3 to regroup and subtract the numbers.
>
> **Step 3** ⟶ Subtract and regroup as needed.

$$\begin{array}{r} {}^{5\ 10\ 12\ 1}\!\!\!\\ \cancel{61.30} \\ -\ 2.89 \\ \hline 58.41 \end{array}$$

Directions: Identify the place value of the underlined number in problems 1–10. For problems 11–15, write the words in decimal form.

1. 7.<u>7</u> _____

2. <u>8</u>.30 _____

3. 0.1<u>8</u>7 _____

4. 3.<u>1</u>98 _____

5. 0.17<u>3</u> _____

6. 7.<u>0</u>1 _____

7. 8.3<u>4</u>5 _____

8. 1<u>1</u>3.1 _____

9. 32.0<u>3</u> _____

10. <u>1</u>23.098 _____

11. 923 thousandths _____

12. 8 tenths _____

13. 34 and 7568 ten-thousandths

_____

14. 152 and 17 thousandths

_____

15. 9 hundredths _____

Directions: Order the decimals from least to greatest.

16. 0.07, 0.77, 0.76 _____

17. 8.801, 4.2509, 4.011 _____

18. 2.34, 23.4, 2.351 _____

19. 3.4, 0.43, 43.304 _____

20. 6.21, 6.23, 6.2123 _____

21. 2.58, 25.835, 25.83596, 258.83596 _____

22. 3.26, 3.19, 3.07, 3.70 _____

23. 24.051, 42.015, 24.060, 24.560 _____

24. 9.345, 93.450, 9.354, 93.540 _____

25. 0.70, 0.77, 7.70, 7.07 _____

Directions: Write >, <, or = to solve each problem.

26. 0.05 ◯ 0.03

27. 0.798 ◯ 0.7968

28. 25.38975 ◯ 253.8975

29. 3.35 ◯ 3.43

30. 0.98568 ◯ 0.998568

31. 4.68 ◯ 6.68

32. 0.78 ◯ 0.780

33. 6.052 ◯ 6. 051

34. 0.012 ◯ 0.01200

35. 36.49 ◯ 36.46

Directions: Add or subtract to solve each problem.

1.	43.5 + 92.1	**7.**	$74.30 $8.65 + $2.50	**13.**	53.97 − 4.24	**19.**	4.2 − 2.7

2.	8.21 + 6.3	**8.**	84.52 + 7.348	**14.**	11.825 − 9.999	**20.**	7.916 − 5.37

3.	25.941 + 6.037	**9.**	62.5 840.1 + 7.3	**15.**	$275.78 − $221.16	**21.**	23,456.56 − 3450.95

4.	$9.75 + $32.94	**10.**	7.201 + 6.24	**16.**	0.56 − 0.37	**22.**	562.867 + 251.78

5.	4.21 + 63.82	**11.**	89.29 − 7.53	**17.**	26.537 − 6.841	**23.**	18,677.88 + 34.20

6.	6.931 + 7.482	**12.**	4.65 − 3.82	**18.**	5.67 − 4.28	**24.**	1,234.678 − 689.240

Facts to Know

You multiply and divide decimals the same way you multiply and divide whole numbers. The difference is that you must be careful to correctly place the decimal point in the product for multiplication and in the quotient for division.

Multiplying with Decimals

Multiplying decimals is the same as multiplying whole numbers. The key is to count the decimal places in each factor.

Sample: 458 x 7.3 = ?

Step 1 → Line up the digits.

$$\begin{array}{r} 458 \\ \times\ 7.3 \\ \hline \end{array}$$

Step 2 → Multiply as with whole numbers.

$$\begin{array}{r} 458 \\ \times\ 7.3 \\ \hline 1374 \\ +\ 32060 \\ \hline 33{,}434 \end{array}$$

Step 3 → Count the decimal places in each factor. The product has the same number of decimal places.

$$\begin{array}{r} 458 \\ \times\ 7.3 \\ \hline 1374 \\ +\ 32060 \\ \hline 3343.4 \end{array}$$

number of decimal places

(1)

Remember, the product has the same number of decimal places as the factors. Sometimes you have to add zeros as needed.

Sample: 2.145 x 0.0321

Step 1	Step 2	Step 3	
2.145	2.145	2.145	*number of decimal places*
x 0.0321	x 0.0321	x 0.0321	
2145	2145	2145	(3)
	42900	42900	+ (4)
		+ 643500	(7)
		0.0688545	

Facts to Know

Multiplying and Dividing with Multiples of 10

You can use shortcuts when you multiply or divide by powers of 10:

- Multiplying by 10
  Move the decimal point 1 place to the right.
  $$3.63 \times 10 = ? \longrightarrow 3.63 \times 10 = 36.3$$

- Multiplying by 100
  Move the decimal point 2 places to the right.
  $$3.63 \times 100 = ? \longrightarrow 3.63 \times 100 = 363.0$$

- Multiplying by 1000
  Move the decimal point 3 places to the right.
  $$3.63 \times 1000 = ? \longrightarrow 3.63 \times 1000 = 3,630.0$$

- Dividing by 10
  Move the decimal point 1 place to the left.
  $$3.63 \div 10 = ? \longrightarrow 3.63 \div 10 = .363$$

- Dividing by 100
  Move the decimal place 2 places to the left. Add a zero for the tenths place.
  $$3.63 \div 100 = ? \longrightarrow 3.63 \div 100 = 0.0363$$

- Dividing by 1000
  Move the decimal point 3 places to the left. Add two zeros for the tenths and hundredths place.
  $$3.63 \div 1000 = ? \longrightarrow 3.63 \div 1000 = 0.00363$$

Dividing with Decimals

Dividing decimals by whole numbers is simple if you place the decimal point in the quotient first.

Sample: $5.95 \div 7 = ?$

Step 1 ⟶ Rewrite the problem and place
the decimal in the quotient.

Step 2 ⟶ Divide and regroup, as needed.

$$
\begin{array}{r}
.85 \\
7\overline{)5.95} \\
-\ 5\ 6\!\downarrow \\
\hline
35 \\
-\ 35 \\
\hline
0
\end{array}
$$

Facts to Know

Dividing with Decimals *(cont.)*

Dividing decimals by decimals means you must move the decimal point by multiplying the divisor and the dividend by the same power of 10 to make the divisor a whole number.

Sample: 20.8 ÷ 2.6 = ?

Because both the dividend and the divisor are numbers with decimals, multiply the divisor and dividend by 10 (since each number has a digit in the tenths place). This makes each number a whole number before you begin dividing. Divide 208 by 26.

$$20.8 \times 10 = 208$$
$$2.6 \times 10 = 26$$

$$
\begin{array}{r}
8 \\
26 \overline{)\,208} \\
-\,208 \\
\hline
0
\end{array}
$$

Sample: 24.00 ÷ 0.13

Because both the dividend and divisor are numbers with decimals, multiply the divisor and dividend by 100 (since each number has a digit in the hundredths place). This makes each number a whole number before you begin dividing). Divide 2400 by 13.

$$24.00 \times 100 = 2400$$
$$0.13 \times 100 = 13$$

$$
\begin{array}{r}
184 \ \text{R8} \\
13 \overline{)\,2400} \\
-\,13\downarrow \\
\hline
110 \\
-\,104\downarrow \\
\hline
60 \\
-\,52 \\
\hline
8
\end{array}
$$

Rounding Decimals

You can round decimals the same way you round whole numbers.

Rule: Remember, if the digit is 5 or greater, round up. If the digit is less than 5, round down.

- Rounding to the nearest whole number

    67.3 →The 3, which is the first number after a whole number, is less than 5. Round to 67.

- Rounding to the nearest tenth

    67. 37 →The 7, which is the first number after the tenths place, is greater than 5. Round to 67.4.

- Rounding to the nearest hundredth

    67. 348 →The 8, which is the first number after the hundredths place, is greater than 5. Round up to 67.35.

Directions: Multiply to solve each problem.

1.	0.84 x 3.15	5.	$10.50 x 0.60	9.	$5.58 x 1.5
2.	2.08 x 0.9	6.	47.8 x 0.1	10.	0.14 x 0.87
3.	0.28 x 9.51	7.	14.2 x 9.7	11.	$1.17 x 21
4.	0.0076 x 0.30	8.	$5.75 x 0.24	12.	8.75 x 0.03

Directions: Divide to solve each problem.

13. $6 \overline{) 3.54}$ 17. $0.06 \overline{) 0.72}$

14. $16 \overline{) 9.12}$ 18. $0.05 \overline{) 7.45}$

15. $12 \overline{) 1.32}$ 19. $0.002 \overline{) 0.688}$

16. $0.40 \overline{) 0.96}$ 20. $0.55 \overline{) 35.31}$

Facts to Know

You can hear how decimals are like fractions. Say a decimal out loud. It sounds like a fraction.

$$0.30 \rightarrow \frac{30}{100} \rightarrow \textbf{thirty hundredths}$$

In the same way, **percent** means per hundred. Hundredths or percents can be used for the same number.

$$\frac{50}{100} = .50 = 50\% \text{ or}$$

There are two ways to change fractions to decimals.

✦ Rewrite the fraction to make its denominator a decimal equivalent in tenths, hundredths, or thousandths.

Sample A: Change $\frac{1}{2}$ to a decimal.

Multiply the numerator and denominator of the fraction by the same number so the denominator comes out as a tenth, hundredth, or thousandth.

Step 1 →Multiply $\frac{1}{2}$ by $\frac{5}{5}$ (1) so the result is a denominator as a tenth.

$$\frac{1}{2} \times \frac{5}{5} = \frac{5}{10}$$

Step 2 →Rewrite $\frac{5}{10}$ as a decimal.

$$\frac{5}{10} = 10\overline{)5.0} \quad \frac{.5}{} = 0.5 \\ \underline{-5\,0}$$

Sample B: Change $\frac{3}{4}$ to a decimal.

Step 1 →Multiply $\frac{3}{4}$ by $\frac{25}{25}$ (1) so the result is a denominator as a hundredth.

$$\frac{3}{4} \times \frac{25}{25} = \frac{75}{100}$$

Step 2 →Rewrite $\frac{3}{4}$ as a decimal.

$$\frac{75}{100} = 100\overline{)75.00} \quad \frac{.75}{} = 0.75 \\ \underline{-700} \\ 500 \\ \underline{-500} \\ 0$$

Facts to Know

✦ For fractions whose denominators are not equivalent to tenths, hundredths, or thousandths, divide the numerator by the denominator.

Sample: Change $\frac{1}{3}$ to a decimal.

Step 1 ⟶ Add a decimal point after the numerator and add two zeros.

$$3\overline{)1.00}$$

Step 2 ⟶ Divide the numerator by the denominator. (In cases where the decimal repeats, put a bar over it.)

$$\begin{array}{r} .33 \\ 3\overline{)1.00} \\ -9\!\downarrow \\ \hline 10 \\ -9 \\ \hline 1 \end{array} = .33\frac{1}{3}$$

Step 3 ⟶ *Optional:* Write the remainder as a fraction.

Look at the figure on the right. It is divided into five equal parts, and two parts are shaded.

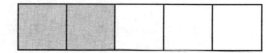

Two of the five squares are shaded. We say "The ratio of shaded to total number of squares is 2 to 5."

Percent is a ratio of some number to 100. Percent means "per hundred." The symbol for percent is %. For example, if there are 40 shaded squares out of 100 total (a ratio of 40 to 100), we would say "40% are shaded."

Percent is often used with money. For example, what is 25% of $2.00? The question that you are really trying to answer is, "what is $\frac{1}{4}$ of $2.00?" because you know that 25% = $\frac{25}{100}$ = $\frac{1}{4}$. The answer is $.50.

Changing a decimal to a percent requires that you change the decimal to hundredths first. You can do this in one of two ways.

✦ Change the decimal to an equivalent fraction.

Sample: Change .7 to a percent.

$$0.7 = \frac{7}{10}$$

Step 1 ⟶ Write the decimal as a fraction.

Step 2 ⟶ If necessary, change the fraction to an equivalent fraction with a denominator of 100. (Remember, percent means "per hundred.")

$$\frac{7}{10} \times \frac{10}{10} = \frac{70}{100}$$

Step 3 ⟶ Change the fraction to a percent.

$$\frac{70}{100} = 70\%$$

Facts to Know

✦ Move the decimal point two places to the right, and include the percent sign. This is the same as multiplying the decimal by a 100.

Sample: Change .7 to a percent ⟶ **.70 = 70%**

There are two ways to change fractions to percents. The first is to change the fraction to an equivalent fraction with a denominator of 100. The second, for fractions that cannot be changed to equivalent fractions with denominators of 100, is to change the fraction to a decimal and then from a decimal to a percent.

✦ Change the fraction to a percent using an equivalent fraction.

Sample: Change $\frac{2}{5}$ to a percent.

Step 1 ⟶ If the denominator of the fraction is a factor of 100, change the fraction to an equivalent fraction with a denominator of 100.

$$\frac{2}{5} \times \frac{20}{20} = \frac{40}{100}$$

Step 2 ⟶ Change the new fraction to a percent.

$$\frac{40}{100} = 40\%$$

✦ Change the fraction to a percent using the decimal method.

Sample: Change $\frac{4}{9}$ to a percent.

Step 1 ⟶ For fractions whose denominators are not factors of 100, divide the numerator by the denominator. Add a decimal point and two zeros.

$$\frac{4}{9} \quad 9\overline{)\begin{array}{r} .44 \\ 4.00 \\ -3\,6\downarrow \\ \hline 40 \\ -36 \\ \hline 4 \end{array}}$$

Step 2 ⟶ Divide. Write any remainder as a fraction.

Step 3 ⟶ Change the decimal to a percent.

$$.44\frac{4}{9} = 44\frac{4}{9}\%$$

Directions: For problems 1–5, write the fraction as a decimal. For problems 6–10, write the decimal as a fraction. For problems 11–15, write the decimal as a fraction in lowest terms.

1. $\frac{7}{10}$ = _____

2. $\frac{2}{5}$ = _____

3. $\frac{3}{4}$ = _____

4. $\frac{3}{20}$ = _____

5. $1\frac{3}{4}$ = _____

6. 0.26 = _____

7. 0.03 = _____

8. 0.2 = _____

9. 0.78 = _____

10. 0.825 = _____

11. 0.05 = _____

12. 0.02 = _____

13. 0.125 = _____

14. 0.04 = _____

15. 6.9 = _____

Directions: Write each as a decimal and a percent.

	decimal	percent
16. six hundredths	_____	_____
17. seventy hundredths	_____	_____
18. 63 per hundred	_____	_____
19. 3 out of 100	_____	_____
20. thirty-one hundredths	_____	_____

Directions: Complete the table.

	percent	fraction	decimal
21.	25%		
22.	2%		
23.	0.5%		
24.	33%		
25.	40%		

Facts to Know

Percent problems usually come as three basic questions:

> • **What is the percent of a number?**
>
> • **What percent is one number of another?**
>
> • **What is a number when a percent is known?**

Because percent means "per hundred," you should always restate any percent problem in terms of decimals or common fractions. That way, you can solve it as a decimal or fraction problem.

Sample A

The school principal said that only 4% of two classes totaling 50 students will be awarded tickets to a baseball game. How many students will receive tickets? (In other words, you want to find 4/100 of 50.)

As a fraction $4\% = \dfrac{4}{100}$

Step 1 →Change 4% to a common fraction or decimal.

or

As a decimal $4\% = .04$

Step 2 →Multiply 50 by the fraction that 4% represents.

$$\dfrac{4}{100} \times \dfrac{50}{1} = \dfrac{200}{100} = 2$$

or

$$.04 \times 50 = 2$$

So 4% of 50 is 2. There are 2 students who will receive tickets.

Sample B: 10% of $70 is ?

Step 1 →Change 10% to a common fraction or decimal. Since the problem involves money, you may want to use the decimal equivalent in this case.

$$10\% = \dfrac{10}{100} = \dfrac{1}{10} = .10$$

Step 2 →Multiply $70 by the decimal equivalent of 10%, which is .10.

$$.10 \times \$70 = \$7$$

Therefore, 10% of $70 is $7.

Facts to Know

Next, suppose one of the factors in a problem is a fraction. Look at the problem $30 = ? \times \frac{1}{4}$. You can find the missing factor by dividing 30 by $\frac{1}{4}$. (Remember to use the reciprocal of the fraction $\frac{1}{4}$ and multiply.):

$$30 \div \frac{1}{4} = \frac{30}{1} \times \frac{4}{1} = 120$$

Percent means "per hundred" so you can use this process to find what percent one number is of another.

Sample

Mr. Riley is costuming 30 actors for the school play. He needs to have red hats for 15 of them. What percent of 30 is the number 15?

Step 1 → First, write the problem in the form 15 = ? x 30. You can find the missing factor by dividing 15 by 30.

$$15 = ? \times 30$$

$$15 \div 30 = 0.5$$

Step 2 → Change the decimal to a percent. The answer is 15 is 50% of 30.

$$0.5 = 50\%$$

This problem can also be solved by thinking of it as a problem comparing ratios. In other words, to find out what percent of 30 the number 15 is, you are trying to find a number that compares to 100 in the same way that 15 compares to 30. So you are looking for the number that (to 100) expresses the same ratio as the ratio of 15 to 30:

Step 1 → Express the problem as a comparison of ratios.

$$\frac{15}{30} = \frac{?}{100}$$

Step 2 → Multiply using the reciprocal of the fraction that has 100 as a denominator.

$$\frac{15}{30} \times \frac{100}{?} = \frac{1500}{30}$$

Step 3 → Simplify.

$$\frac{1500}{30} = 50$$

So 15 is 50% of 30.

Facts to Know

Here are examples of the steps involved in finding a number when a percent is known.

Sample A

Rudy and Sally are playing a treasure hunt game, and they know that 6 clues have been found. They also know that 6 clues are 25% of all the clues. What is the total number of clues?

You know that 6 is 25% of some number. You can use the process of finding a missing factor to solve this problem.

Step 1 → Write the problem. You know that 25% is 0.25 so the problem can be rewritten. Remember that the decimals in the divisor and dividend need to be moved so you can divide with whole numbers. (Move the decimals the same number of places.)

$$6 = 25\% \times ?$$

$$6 = .25 \times ?$$

$$.25\overline{)6.00}$$

Step 2 → Find the missing factor by dividing 6 by 0.25.

So 6 is 25% of 24.

$$
\begin{array}{r}
24 \\
25\overline{)600} \\
-50 \\
\hline
100 \\
-100 \\
\hline
0
\end{array}
$$

Sample B: 46 is 115% of what number?

$$46 = 115\% \times ?$$

Step 1 → Write the problem. You know that 115% is 1.15 so the problem can be rewritten. Remember that the decimals in the divisor and dividend need to be moved so you can divide with whole numbers. (Move the decimals the same number of places.)

$$1.15\overline{)46.00}$$

Step 2 → Find the missing factor by dividing 46 by 115.

So 46 is 115% of 40.

$$
\begin{array}{r}
40 \\
115\overline{)4600} \\
-460 \\
\hline
0
\end{array}
$$

Directions: Solve the story problems. Remember to restate any percent in terms of a fraction or decimal.

1. On Monday, 100 students arrived on two buses. On Tuesday, many students had the flu, and only 75% of Monday's group arrived at school. How many students had the flu? (**Hint:** You want to find 75/100 of 100.) _____

2. There are 70 advertising signs on the home run fence at the Isaac Walton Baseball Field. A tornado damaged 30% of them and they need to be replaced. How many need to be replaced? _____

3. Two hundred and fifty people are expected to turn out for the 4th of July picnic. Sixty percent of them will be children. How many children will attend? _____

4. Of the 12 girls on the softball team, 25 percent are left-handed. How many are left-handed? _____

5. Four hundred new homes are being built in the town of Frankfort and only 5% have swimming pools. How many have swimming pools? _____

Directions: Solve the problems.

6. 17 is what percent of 340? _____

7. 420 is what percent of 70? _____

8. 60 is what percent of 300? _____

9. 25 is what percent of 150? _____

10. 30 is what percent of 120? _____

11. 16 is 20% of what number? _____

12. 63 is 70% of what number? _____

13. 70 is 110% of what number? _____

14. 13 is 10% of what number? _____

15. 12 Is 14% of what number? _____

16. 30 is 500% of what number? _____

17. 76 is 1% of what number? _____

18. 42 is 18% of what number? _____

Bake Sale

Lauren had 4 cakes to sell at the school bake sale. "I'm going to cut these in half," she thought, "in case someone only wants half."

1. If someone wants a whole cake, how many halves will Lauren sell to the person? _____

2. How many half cakes can Lauren make out of 4 whole cakes? _____

3. Holly sold $\frac{1}{4}$ of a pie to each person who wanted a piece. She had 8 pies and they all were sold. How many people bought pieces of pie? _____

4. Kyle sold nuts: $1\frac{1}{2}$ pounds of walnuts, $\frac{5}{8}$ pound of pecans, and $1\frac{1}{8}$ pounds of peanuts. Did he sell more or less than 3 pounds of nuts? _____

Dollars and Sense

5. There's a sale at the local grocery store.

Tomato Soup → 7 cans for $0.56	Sugar → 5 pounds for $0.45

   How much does 1 can of tomato soup cost? _____ How much does 1 pound of sugar cost? _____

6. The Najera family ate at Heartland Café and the bill was $23.48 for four. They all ordered the same thing! What was the cost of each person's meal? _____

7. Lupe loves to garden. She paid $143.78 for a tree, $53.67 for tulip bulbs, $17.09 for tomato plants, and $11.34 for a bag of grass seed. How much did she spend in all? _____

8. Lauren's dad went on a canoe trip. He spent $37.34 on gas, $264.77 on canoe rental, $127.45 on food, $189.34 on a new sleeping bag, and $47.12 on souvenirs. How much did the trip cost? _____

9. Jessica needs 12 meters of ribbon to make 9 ties. Ribbon costs $0.89 a meter. How much change does she receive from her $20 bill? _____

10. Carson raised $1.85 per kilometer in a charity run. If she ran 20.5 kilometers, how much money did she raise? (Round to nearest hundredth). _____

11. Gabriella worked 16 hours last week and earned $94.40. How much money did she earn per hour? _____

12. Marie babysits after school. She babysat for 15 hours last week and earned $81. How much money did she charge per hour? _____

13. If you buy four 16-ounce cans of chili, they are 4 for $1.00. How much would you spend per ounce? (Round to nearest thousandth.) _____

Lunch!

14. How many servings of $\frac{1}{2}$ a cantaloupe can you make from 2 cantaloupes? _____ from 3 cantaloupes? _____

15. Gabriel had 3 cookies. He gave David $\frac{1}{2}$ of a cookie. How many cookies does Gabriel have left? _____

Simple Word Problems with Fractions and Percents

Directions: Solve the word problems below.

1. The Lincoln Way cheerleaders in Frankfort raised $1,000.00 during the school year.

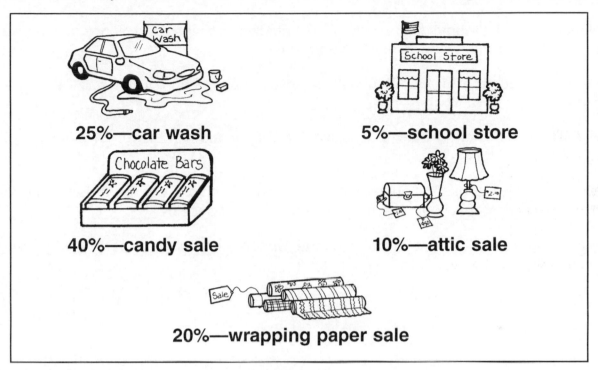

   25%—car wash

   5%—school store

   40%—candy sale

   10%—attic sale

   20%—wrapping paper sale

   a. Which activity collected the most money? _____

   b. Which activity collected the least amount of money? _____

   c. How much did they raise with the candy sale? _____

   d. How much money did they raise with the car wash? _____

   e. How much money did they raise at the school store? _____

2. Mrs. Anderson's Girl Scout troop has $600 in savings. The girls collected 50% of the money by recycling aluminum cans. Fifteen percent of the money came from donations and 35% of it came from their annual auction. How much money was raised by selling cans, donations, and by having an auction? _____

3. Your purchases total $24.95. If the sales tax rate is 6%, what is the total amount that you must pay? (Round to the nearest penny.) _____

4. Art walked $1\frac{1}{4}$ miles Monday, $2\frac{3}{4}$ miles Tuesday, and $1\frac{1}{2}$ miles Wednesday. How many miles did he walk? _____

5. Andrew's dad drove 60 miles per hour to get to the amusement park. It took them 1 hour and 20 minutes. How many miles is it to the amusement park? _____

If you have difficulty solving some of these brain teasers, try drawing the problem. It often helps to picture what's being described.

Number Fun

1. Nancy and Bill ate breakfast at school. Bill ate five pancakes and Nancy ate two fewer than Bill. How many pancakes did Nancy eat? _____

2. Fred is two years older than Paul but six years younger than Bill. If Bill is 24, how old is Fred? _____ Paul? _____

3. Mrs. Thomas cooked two dozen cookies, but Tad ate eight of them. How many cookies did she have left? _____

4. Mr. O'Leary will cook for eight people on Sunday. If one cup of rice will feed four people, how many cups of rice will she need to cook for eight people? _____

5. If you divided an hour into four equal parts, what do you call each part? _____ How many minutes are there in each part? _____

Magic 3!

Steps	Sample
1. Choose a number.	58
2. Multiply by 3.	58 x 3 = 174
3. Add 1.	174 + 1 = 175
4. Add 1 again.	175 + 1 = 176
5. Now add the three answers you got in steps 2, 3, and 4.	174 + 175 + 176 = 525
6. Add the digits in the sum.	5 + 2 + 5 = 12
7. Keep adding the digits in each sum until a single digit is reached. This will always be 3.	1 + 2 = 3

Try this trick with numbers you choose. Show a friend. Say, "You may select any number that you like. If you do as I say, I will tell you the answer."

Cloud Cover

Help the weather forecaster explain what percent of the sky will be covered by clouds.

Type	Description	Write the Percentages
Clear	Sky has no clouds or clouds cover less than $\frac{1}{10}$ of the sky.	from 0 to 10%
Scattered	An average of $\frac{1}{10}$ to $\frac{5}{10}$ is covered.	
Broken	Clouds covered $\frac{5}{10}$ to $\frac{9}{10}$ of the sky.	
Overcast	Clouds covered $\frac{9}{10}$ of the sky.	

Thanksgiving Puzzle

Can you solve this Thanksgiving puzzle? **T** has been done for you. One of the letters is extra and does not belong in the puzzle.

$$\underset{0}{\underline{\quad\quad}} \quad \underset{1}{\underline{\quad\quad}} \quad \underset{2}{\underline{\quad\quad}} \quad \underset{3}{\underline{\quad\quad}} \quad \underset{4}{\underline{\quad\quad}} \quad \underset{5}{\underline{\quad\quad}} \quad \underset{6}{\underline{\quad T \quad}} \quad \underset{7}{\underline{\quad\quad}}$$

1. T: It is a multiple of 2. It is greater than 3.
2. M: It is greater than ($\frac{10}{5}$). It is less than T − 2.
3. U: It is a multiple of 5. It is greater than M.
4. R = M + T − 1
5. Y: Divide T by M.
6. L: U x L = U
7. O: It is greater than T − M. It is less than 5.
8. H: H − O = M
9. P = U − U

Kite Factory

On a visit to a kite factory, Guadalupe noticed that the kites are made in the following repeated order: dragon, box, bat, fish, tiger, turkey. What will the design be on the 77th kite?

Conduct a Survey and Create a Circle Graph

Directions: Using spreadsheet or graphing software (such as *Microsoft Excel*, etc.), take a survey and show your results on a circle (or pie) graph. Follow the steps in the sample below and modify as needed.

Sample

1. Take a class survey about a topic that you want to ask your classmates about. The sample pie graph is entitled, "What is your favorite type of movie?"

2. Enter your data into a spreadsheet or graphing software program. Remember to enter the percentages in one column and the labels for the different parts of the pie graph in another column.

3. Select the pie graph as the type of graph with which you want to display the results.

4. Print out your pie graph and on another sheet of paper, describe what question was asked during your survey and what results were obtained.

What is your favorite type of movie?

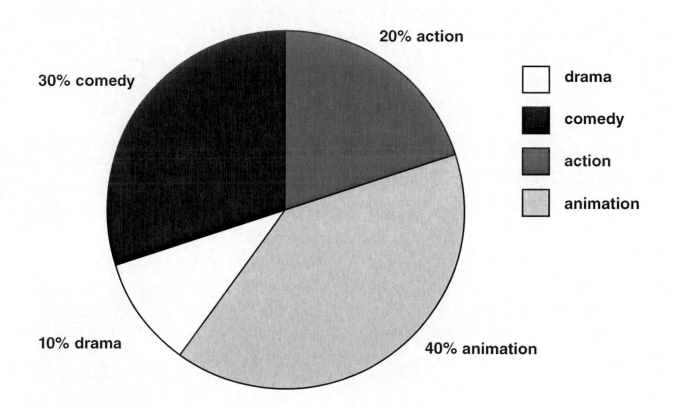

Page 7
1. a. 2/4 or 1/2
   b. whole
2. a. 3/5
   b. group
3. a. 3/6 or 1/2
   b. whole
4. a. 1/4
   b. group
5. 1/7
6. 2/7
7. 1/3
8. 1/2
9. 4/6 or 2/3
10. 3/6 or 1/2

Page 8
1. b
2. a
3. b
4. b
5. c
6. 3, 9
7. 2, 8
8. 6, 12
9. 2, 4
10. 3, 3
11. 8, 1
12. 2, 5
13. a
14. c
15. b

Page 13
1. b
2. d
3. c
4. b
5. a
6. c
7. 2/5
8. 3/4
9. 6/7
10. 2/5
11. 3/4
12. 5/6
13. 1/2
14. 4/5

15. 1/2
16. 10
17. 21
18. 18
19. 24
20. 12
21. 40
22. 7/15
23. 1/2
24. 5/6
25. They are equal.
26. 3/4
27. 7/8
28. a. 6/5
    b. 3 1/4
    c. 2 1/7
    d. 1 2/3
    e. 2 3/8
29. a. 9/4
    b. 20/3
    c. 59/8
    d. 7/4
    e. 43/8
30. 3/5
31. 5/4 = 1 1/4
32. 2/8 = 1/4
33. 8/3 = 2 2/3
34. 7/7 = 1
35. 6/5 = 1 1/5

Page 18
1. 4/5
2. 5/7
3. 1/5
4. 5/14
5. 1/4
6. 1/3
7. 1 1/2
8. 1/3
9. 1 2/11
10. 1 3/7
11. 1 1/2
12. 5/8
13. 8 1/3
14. 7
15. 3 1/2
16. 12 1/14

17. 9 2/5
18. like; no; 1 1/3
19. like; yes; 2 1/2
20. unlike; no; 3 11/18

Page 21
1. 1/3
2. 9
3. 4 3/8
4. 2 6/11
5. 3 gallons
6. 1/2 mile
7. 5 teams
8. 9 students
9. 2/15
10. 7/16
11. 8/63
12. 1/8 inch
13. 3/8 of the gallon
14. 1/16 of a mile
15. 1/6 of a mile
16. 3/8 of a cup
17. 5/6
18. 1 3/4
19. 2 1/4
20. 4 1/3
21. 9
22. 2 5/7
23. 4/5
24. 1 9/10
25. 5/12

Page 24
1. 1/3
2. 4/3
3. 1/5
4. 9/8
5. 1/10
6. 1/7
7. 5/4
8. 7/6
9. 1/4
10. 1/17
11. 18
12. 3/20
13. 6
14. 32
15. 6 3/4

16. 3/8
17. 6
18. 25
19. 1/21
20. 4 1/2
21. 1/32
22. 11/60
23. 7/24
24. 32 1/2
25. 4 2/3
26. 7 5/7
27. 5/13
28. 1/20
29. 12
30. 1/12

Page 25
1. 5/6
2. 4/9
3. 15/16
4. 2 4/7
5. 2/5
6. 4
7. 1/2
8. 1
9. 4
10. 2 1/3
11. 2/3
12. 1 21/25
13. 1 37/40
14. 2 3/10
15. 1 7/10
16. 2 1/14
17. 1 9/14
18. 3 1/18
19. 96/125
20. 11/12

Page 28
1. tenths
2. ones
3. hundredths
4. tenths
5. thousandths
6. tenths
7. hundredths
8. tens
9. hundredths

10. hundreds
11. 0.923
12. 0.8
13. 34.7568
14. 152.017
15. 0.09
16. 0.07, 0.76, 0.77
17. 4.011, 4.2509, 8.801
18. 2.34, 2.351, 23.4
19. 0.43, 3.4, 43.304
20. 6.21, 6.2123, 6.23
21. 2.58, 25.835, 25.83596, 258.83596
22. 3.07, 3.19, 3.26, 3.70
23. 24.051, 24.060, 24.560, 42.015
24. 9.345, 9.354, 93.450, 93.540
25. 0.70, 0.77, 7.07, 7.70
26. >
27. >
28. <
29. <
30. <
31. <
32. =
33. >
34. =
35. >

Page 29
1. 135.6
2. 14.51
3. 31.978
4. $42.69
5. 68.03
6. 14.413
7. $85.45
8. 91.868
9. 909.9
10. 13.441
11. 81.76
12. 0.83

13. 49.73
14. 1.826
15. $54.62
16. 0.19
17. 19.696
18. 1.39
19. 1.5
20. 2.546
21. 20,005.61
22. 814.647
23. 18,712.08
24. 545.438

Page 33
1. 2.646
2. 1.872
3. 2.6628
4. 0.00228
5. $6.30
6. 4.78
7. 137.74
8. $1.38
9. $8.37
10. 0.1218
11. 24.57
12. 0.2625
13. 0.59
14. 0.57
15. 0.11
16. 2.4
17. 12
18. 149
19. 344
20. 64.2

Page 37
1. 0.7
2. 0.4
3. 0.75
4. 0.15
5. 1.75
6. 26/100
7. 3/100
8. 2/10
9. 78/100
10. 825/1000
11. 1/20
12. 1/50

13. 1/8
14. 1/25
15. 6 9/10
16. .06, 6%
17. .70, 70%
18. .63, 63%
19. .03, 3%
20. .31, 31%
21. 25/100, 0.25
22. 2/100, 0.02
23. 0.5/100 or 5/1000, 0.005
24. 33/100, 0.333
25. 40/100, .40

Page 41
1. 25
2. 21
3. 150
4. 3
5. 20
6. 5%
7. 600%
8. 20%
9. 16.7%
10. 25%
11. 80
12. 90
13. 63.64
14. 130
15. 85.71
16. 6
17. 7,600
18. $233.\overline{3}$

Pages 42
1. 2
2. 8
3. 32
4. more than (3.25 lbs.)
5. $.08, $.09
6. $5.87
7. $225.88
8. $666.02
9. $9.32
10. $37.93
11. $5.90

12. $5.40
13. $0.016
14. 4, 6
15. 21/2

Page 43
1. a. candy sale
   b. school store
   c. $400.00
   d. $250.00
   e. $50.00
2. $300.00, $90.00, $210.00
3. $26.45
4. 5 1/2 miles
5. 80 miles

Pages 44

Number Fun
1. 3
2. Fred is 18, Paul is 16.
3. 16
4. 2
5. a quarter; 15 min

Pages 45

Cloud Cover
10%–50%
50%–90%
90%

Thanksgiving Puzzle
PLYMOUTH

Kite Factory
Tiger